Preface
Kerry Hardie

The places may be real but the people aren't, of that I am certain. Neither are the wives, widows, mothers, stepmothers, girlfriends, sisters, daughters and grandmothers. Not forgetting the long-suffering aunts. Still, it's good to see the feminine acknowledged and included. Sometimes men seem to labour under the illusion that they create themselves. Which they don't. Unless they're writers or illusionists. Having just stepped out of the luminous and fantastical world of Bruno Schulz's *The Street of Crocodiles*, it is easy to step into Gabriel Rosenstock's equally fantastical world of the men he has met and the things they have told him. These men have grown themselves out of their places of origin, they have sprouted tall like sunflowers, or bushed out into spikey pyrocanthus or crawled along the ground like dead nettle. Once grown, Rosenstock seems to have little control over them, and they run him around in a merry dance that submits to nothing but rhythm and rhyme and the joy of their self-invention.

I don't like limericks and I don't get nonsense verse, and if some child, solemn-faced, presents me with a riddle that I don't already know the answer to, then trying to unriddle it is like some arcane form of torture. But I like these men of Rosenstock's, they make me laugh, they make me reach for the atlas and spread it out on the floor, then pore, bottom-up and magnifying glass in hand, through indexes and countries I have hardly even heard of.

Of course, they are much cleverer than I am so often I don't get the sub-text straight away. I'm alright on the man from the Ivory Coast who thinks he's a ghost, or the man from Pondicherry who years ago drank himself to death on sherry, but mostly I have to wait for the penny to drop or ask my husband who knows things, or simply 'goa with the [delightful] floa', which I am more than happy to do.

I met a man from Kitty Hawk,
Himself and the wife were like cheese and chalk,
His dog used to bring him out for a walk –
  Just to talk

I met a man from Mozambique,
Says I to him, 'I need a leak.'
He looked at me, 'You some kind of freak?'
I tried to explain – it took a week

I met a man from the North Cape
His hair was wild, his mouth agape:
At four in the morning he'd peel a grape –
I have that eerie sound on tape

I met a man from Ballinamuck
And all he had in the world was a duck;
One night it drowned – what rotten luck!
That duckless man from Ballinamuck

POETRY LIBRARY

I met a man from John O' Groats
Wearing forty overcoats.
'Stay warm!' he muttered, 'Eat your oats!'
  How he gloats

I met a man from Kara-Kum,
A dosser, a hobo, a flea-bitten bum.
What did he sell for some chewing gum?
  His mum

I met a man from Zottegem
'Oh no!' says I, 'Not him again!'
He then coughed up a lot of phlegm –
    Ahem!

I met a man from Wolf Creek,
I said, 'How do?' He said, 'Don't speak!
Abide in silence – for one week
    Shut the beak!'

I met a man from the Isle of Man
And he said, 'Catch me if you can!'
He ran and ran and ran and ran
  And – damn that man!

I met a man from the Gulf of Kutch
Who nattered on about such and such;
He had nothing to say – well, not very much ...
As he lived in a tiny rabbit hutch

I met a man from San Miguel
Who had a sign: NOTHING TO SELL.
How can he live? 'Amigo, it's hell!'
  He wasn't well ...

I met a man from Reykjavik
Nearly bald – his neck was thick.
His only rib of hair combed slick –
His head all shiny – like a brick

I met a man from Simplon Pass
Who built a memorial made of brass
Not to himself – but to his ass –
    (How crass)

I met a man from Zwartemeer
Which is in Holland, (should you care):
I think he is no longer there –
  Where?

I met a man from Yaibra Shan
Who said, 'It's me! Your greatest fan!
Oh please allow me carry your can!'
  Uncanny man

I met a man from sunny France
Who wore a kilt instead of a pants:
Mon dieu! You should have seen him dance
  (Worth a glance)

I met a man from Kalamazoo
Who claimed he had a cure for the flu:
'Stick all them germs together with glue!'
  Whoo!

I met a man from Pallas Green
He showed me his liver, then his spleen:
'See what happens when you drink potheen?
  You lose your sheen!'

POETRY LIBRARY

I met a man in Purwodadi
Who said 'I'd like to be your caddy!'
'What shall I call you, then, my laddie?'
'I'm Paddy the caddy from Purwodadi!'

I met a man from Agramunt,
Even his friends used to call him a runt.
'Well ... somebody's got to bear the brunt!'
  Said he, with a grunt

I met a man from Maseru
Who said in Sesotho, 'What! You too!'
Just like that – out of the blue!
'Who,' I sighed, ' who – who are you?'

I met a man in Pondicherry
'Yes, I'm alive, now – very, very!
Years ago I lived in Kerry ...
Drank myself to death on sherry!'

I met a man in old Bangkok,
A doctor, 'Hey, come here old stock!
You wanna buy a smelly sock?'
    'Er, no thanks, doc'

I met a man from Kurdistan,
He'd heard of Oliver but not of Stan!
(He was Oliver's greatest living fan)
  A hardy man

I met a man from the Alamo,
One word he had and that was 'No!'
Could hardly hear him, he spoke so low,
  'Didn't catch that, bro'?'

I met a man in Vatican City
Dressed as a nun and singing a ditty,
The chorus was, 'I'm sitting pretty ...
Let's get down to the nitty gritty!'

I met a man from Safid Kūh
Slowly sipping morning dew:
'I take it weekdays for the flu ...
Also – not a bad shampoo!'

I met a man from Botany Bay
Who said: 'Good night! I mean good day!
Er, good morning's what I meant to say!'
    'Well, OK ...'

I met a man from Veracruz
A gambler, he was born to lose:
He lost his shirt, his drawers, his shoes
  Then hit the booze

POETRY LIBRARY

I met a man from Côte d'Or
In a Turkish bath at half past four;
His skin was opening ... pore by pore
And more and more and more and more

I met a man from Arrandale
Who had a plan – it couldn't fail!
I'm afraid it did, he's now in jail
  Growing pale

I met a man from a place called Bale
'Have I,' says he, 'a very strange tale!
He had – he wiggled it ! I grew pale ...
It was for sale

I met a man from Diyarbakir
Who came too close with a leering leer:
I said in Kurdish, 'Your beard's in my beer!'
As into my glass he shed a tear

I met a man from Unapool
Whose nose was very, very cool:
He iced his Scotch with it – the fool!
   A ghoul

I met a man from Wollongong,
I asked him would he sing a song
'You know I always get it wrong:
Something –something – pinga-ding dong'

I met a man from Vietnam
Who said his name was 'Auntie Sam',
He was as gentle as a lamb
Always sat at the back of the tram

I met a man from the town of Wynne,
Picking his nose he said, with a grin,
'It may not be nice – but is it a sin?
   Goes well with gin ...'

I met a man from old Nan Ling
Who bought a lark that couldn't sing;
He boiled and ate the wretched thing
   Then threw me a wing

I met a man from Kathmandou
Who sneezed and said, 'I am the flu!'
His nose was broken – his English too –
'Aaaaaaaaaaaa – oooh– tichou!'

I met a man from the Shetland Isles
Whose beaming face was wreathed in smiles
Which could be seen for miles and miles –
(You'd never think that he had piles)

I met a man from Springfield, Mass.,
An explosive fellow (I'm sure 'twas gas)
He used to say, 'This, too, will pass!'
A neck of brass

I met a man in a town called Punch
(In India) and he bought me lunch
An assortment of nuts – which I tried to munch
  But failed to crunch

I met a man from a town called Price,
At first I thought him awfully nice.
You know, he gave me ALL his lice!
  Not once, twice

POETRY LIBRARY

I met a man on the banks of the Rhine
Reciting his poetry line by line:
I had to put up with his feverish whine:
    'Filthy *schwein!*'

I met a man who had no face
'Twas in New Delhi, in Connaught Place,
He had covered the hole with exquisite lace ...
   A walking pillow case

I met a man from Zhanjiang
Charged with stealing a small meringue:
'I'll die,' he roared, 'I'll fry! I'll hang!'
As on his banjo he did twang

I met a man from Valladolid.
His name was long so I called him Sid.
I shouldn't have, but, then, I did –
He held me up, saying, 'What am I bid?'

I met a man from Singapore
Who really was a crashing bore:
'Would you repeat that???' he would roar
  My brain was sore

I met a man from Rapid River
Fishing for trout with bits of liver
(His own): 'I've nothin' left to give her!'
  He began to shiver

I met a man from Aquitaine
In a meadow drinking rain
Quite convinced it was champagne –
  Pea–brain

I met a man near the North Pole
And he went searching for his soul:
'Must have fallen down that hole
  Life takes its toll!'

I met a man from Kinder Scout:
'I'd love to be a lager lout!'
Alas! He's suffering from the gout
Wont' go out, does nothing but pout

I met a man from Zonguldak
On route to Lhasa on his yak:
Once a week he'd give it a whack –
  Then rub its back

I met a man near the Eiffel Tower
He kindly handed me a flower
It withered after half an hour –
  A spy gone sour?

POETRY LIBRARY

I met a man from Santa Fé
With thirty bills he couldn't pay;
Last I heard he'd learned to pray
For what, to whom? I cannot say

I met a man from Nunavut
An Inuit in a verbal rut:
'But ...' he would say. 'But what??' 'But ...'
  A bit of a nut

I met a man from South Korea
Who had a dose of diarrhoea:
'Bye bye,' he said, 'Good luck! I'll see ya!
One day – you'll see – I'll be a ... be a – '

I met a man from Montserrat
Who said he dabbled in 'dis an' dat' –
Was he de rat who stole me hat?
   De brat!

I met a man in old Siam
Who simply said, 'I am, you am!'
His job was catching wasps in jam
  Bam! Bam!

I met a man from Ecuador
Who went to bed and tried to snore
All he could do was yelp and roar:
   'Four!'

I met a man from Werris Creek,
His past was dull, his outlook bleak:
'Things might look up,' he said, 'next week ...'
   A geek

I met a man from the Pyrenees
Who drinks white wine with anti-freeze –
Preventing icicles when he pees –
    If you please

I met a man from good old Goa,
There since the Flood – his name is Noah:
'You gotta goa with the floa!'
    'Whoa!'

I met a man and it was dark
We hunted together in Emu Park
All of a sudden he started to bark:
'Watch out for the shark! Hark! Hark! The lark!'

I met a man from East Berlin
Sitting in his rubbish bin.
'Mein Herr!' he said, with an awful grin,
   'No one's in!'

I met a man from Bangalore
Whose mantra was, 'Encore! Encore!'
That's all I knew of him – no more –
   A man to the fore

I met a man from Stoke-on-Trent
Who'd only a penny – and that was bent;
Next thing I heard ... it, too, was spent,
   (Wherever it went)

I met a man inside a room
I think it was in El Khartûm
He said, 'Beware the Hour of Doom!'
And floored me with a shadowy broom

POETRY LIBRARY

I met a man from the Vale of York
Who hated wine – but loved the cork
Which he would eat with knife and fork
  A dork

I met a man from the Bahamas
Who kept live fish in his pyjamas
For breakfast he had stewed pirhanas –
Served in style by two pet llamas

I met a man from Tenerife
A vegetarian, he looked like a leaf,
At dinner he would cry, 'Good grief!
  Where's the beef?'

I met a man from Ivory Coast
Who used to boast he was a ghost:
No noise he made when munching toast
Opening up his morning post

I met a man from old Darjeeling,
For twenty years he had been kneeling –
'At last!' he cried, 'I have no feeling!'
Up he leaped – and hit the ceiling

I met a man from West Bengal
A drunkard – only three feet tall.
He fell from grace – oh, what a fall!
   That's all

Also available from DOGHOUSE:

Heart of Kerry -- an anthology of writing
from performers at Poet's Corner, Harty's Bar, Tralee 1992-2003

Song of the Midnight Fox - Eileen Sheehan

Loose Head & Other Stories - Tommy Frank O'Connor

Both Sides Now - Peter Keane

Shadows Bloom / Scáthanna Faoi Bhláth - haiku by John W.
Sexton, translations into Irish by Gabriel Rosenstock

FINGERPRINTS (On Canvas) - Karen O'Connor

Vortex - John W. Sexton

The Waiting Room - Margaret Galvin

Apples in Winter - Liam Aungier

The Doghouse Book of **Ballad Poems**

Every DOGHOUSE book costs €12, postage free, to anywhere in the
world (& other known planets). Cheques, Postal Orders (or any legal
method) payable to DOGHOUSE,
also PAYPAL (www.paypal.com) to doghousepaypal@eircom.net

*"Buy a full set of DOGHOUSE books, in time they will be
collectors items"* **- Gabriel Fitzmaurice, April 12, 2005.**

DOGHOUSE
P.O. Box 312
Tralee G.P.O.
Tralee
Co. Kerry
Ireland
tel + 353 6671 37547
email doghouse312@eircom.net   www.doghousebooks.ie